SISTERHOOD & SEASONS

Sisterhood & Seasons Workbook
Reflections and Practices
for the Seasons of Black Women's Friendships

Stephanie C. Burton, MSEd, LMHC

A SoulFull by Design Book

Cover and interior design and formatting by Stephanie C. Burton | SoulFull by Design

Copyeditor: Crystal Nero

ISBN: 979-8-218-82819-6

To keep up to date on Stephanie C. Burton's writings, please visit her website: www.soulfullbydesign.com

To my sister-friends.

Thank you. I love you.

CONTENTS

· · · · · · · · · · ·

PART THREE: Spring — No Shade, Just Growth

PART FOUR: Summer — Reunions, Second Chances, and Self-Care

CONCLUSION

LETTER TO THE READER

DEAR SIS,

In my own life, friendship with other Black women has been one of my most significant sources of joy and encouragement. It has been a rock in weary seasons. It has felt like a blessed baptism into Black womanhood, offering warmth when the world around us turns cold. Yet, within its beauty, there have also been ashes—fallouts, tears, heartbreaks, and disappointments.

Just as the seasons change, our friendships can shift over time. These lived experiences, together with my clinical work, have led me to write this book. I know these experiences are not just mine—they are pretty common—but they can feel so isolating because we rarely talk about the pain of friendship wounds, or the process of rebuilding these kinds of relationships. The friendship between Black women deserves this kind of care and attention.

We thrive in community—it is where we laugh, grow, cry, and rise to be our best selves. So, when the group chat gets quiet, or something in the vibe just feels off, it's OK to pause and check in with the friendship, and with yourself. These moments do not always mean the love is gone, but they might indicate that the season is changing.

In those shifts, we can practice showing up with tenderness. We can learn to honor the season without losing the sister or losing ourselves. We can learn to tell the truth without breaking the bond. And when needed, we can learn to gently grieve what has changed, and let go—even if it once felt like forever. In the eloquent words of Dr. Joy Harden Bradford, author of, *Sisterhood Heals: The Transformative Power of Healing in Community*, "Sometimes, we need to sit in the discomfort to get to the other side of pain. Sometimes there is no peace in the moment and that has got to be OK." A critical part of healing our friendships and the wounds the breakups cause is trusting ourselves to sit with the pain and reach the other side of it; with our mind, body, and soul still intact.

In this book I have taken intentional care to include friendship topics, reflections, and activities that are relatable and healing. Within these pages, you will find:

- Themes and experiences that reflect some of the ups and downs of friendship between Black women.
- Clinical perspective that explores how our shared history and lived experience shape how we connect, while naming the sometimes hard-to-define challenges of friendship with therapeutic insight and care.
- Reflection tools and exercises to name what is hard, celebrate what is treasured, and restore what is worth saving.
- Affirmations that uplift and encourage.
- Tracks from my personal playlist to set the tone.

Whether you are moving through this book solo or with a circle of friends doing some healing together, go at your own pace. Flip to the section that fits your moment, or take the journey from start to finish. While it is backed by therapeutic insight that I often use with my therapy clients, this book is not a substitute for therapy. You may need to consult with a licensed mental health counselor in your area if you notice some deeper issues that arise or that feel difficult to process on your own or with your friends. If you find that this rings true for you and you are looking for a therapist, I highly recommend checking out the Therapist Directory, specially curated for Black women by Dr. Joy Harden Bradford: www.therapyforblackgirls.com.

Here's to healing, honoring, and holding our sisterhood experiences with softness, truth, and love.

From my heart to yours,

It seems to me that trying to live without friends is like milking a bear to get cream for your morning coffee. It is a whole lot of trouble, and then not worth much after you get it.

- Zora Neale Hurston, Anthropologist, Folklorist, Writer, and Filmmaker

INTRODUCTION

The Inheritance of Sisterhood

It matters to me that anyone who reads this book understands the lens through which I see friendship—especially friendship between Black women—and why I cherish it so much.

For centuries, we as Black women have been each other's keepers. In the Bantu tradition, the concept of *ubuntu*—I am because we are—shaped how our ancestors understood relationships. Community was not optional; it was the heartbeat of survival. To me, this deeply resonates with my own perspective on all of the various relationships we have with one another. Ubuntu explains why our best friends become sisters, and why godmothers and "play aunties" are just as real as blood relatives. We come from an inheritance of kinship that built thriving villages and powerful kingdoms.

That same spirit sheltered us through the brutal dislocation of the Transatlantic Slave Trade. Even in the dehumanizing system of slavery, Black women found ways to nurture and protect one another—sharing food, nurturing and watching over each other's children, passing down songs and wisdom to keep our spirits lifted in the midst of unimaginable turmoil. During the Reconstruction and Jim Crow eras, we passed along survival strategies, economic opportunities, and even beauty secrets—such as Madam C.J. Walker's hair care formulas—through word of mouth. We taught each other how to dream out loud, to stand up for ourselves, and to face our fears head-on. We formed sororities, federated women's clubs, auxiliaries, and other organizations centered on our innate need and desire to lean on one another as we face the world before us. We have walked together in protest, sat together in grief, and laughed together at kitchen tables and in beauty shops, owning joy as our birthright.

This is the legacy we carry: a sisterhood that has not only endured, but has carried us through generations. Nevertheless, that depth comes with its own complexities. When our friendships strain, it can feel personal, even earth-shattering, because these ties become so closely connected to our identity, safety, and sense of belonging. A single bend in the bond can feel like a fracture in the ground beneath us, leaving us holding pieces that we are unsure how to fit back together.

In the seasons of our sisterhood, some friendships blossom, some fade away, and some shift into entirely new shapes. We need to name these seasons, navigate them with care, and strengthen the bonds that are meant to last. It is about protecting our heritage of sisterhood so that the next generation inherits not only our resilience, but also our tenderness toward one another. It is also essential to recognize that tenderness does not have to be conditional upon whether or not the friendship survives. We can still be gentle with our sisters and with ourselves, even when we are no longer in relationships with them.

The Science of Friendship

Friendship is so profoundly connected to our physical, emotional, mental, and spiritual health. Scientists in psychology and public health consistently inform us that strong, supportive relationships reduce the risk and symptoms of anxiety, depression, and even cardiovascular disease. Interestingly, cardiovascular disease, according to the American Heart Association, is the number one cause of death among Black women ages 25 and over. That reality gives "the heart of a sister" new meaning—because, heart to heart, if we are not truly caring for one another, we could be contributing to each other's slow decline.

Healthy friendships serve as a buffer against life's stressors. They can lower cortisol—the body's primary stress hormone—boost immune function, and increase resilience in the face of trauma or grief. Close friendships help alleviate symptoms of depression by providing a sense of connection, affirmation, and belonging. Spiritually, friendships remind us of our shared humanity and interconnectedness, creating spaces where our values, dreams, and truths can be witnessed without judgment.

For Black women, this is especially important. Too often, we move through spaces where care and visibility seem scarce. When we do find those nourishing connections, we fight hard to keep them—sometimes even willing to fight each other. This willingness to fight each other can stem from a scarcity mindset, shaping how we view loyalty and the number of "real ones" we believe we can have.

Friendships remind us that we do not have to navigate this world alone. They hold up a mirror to our worth when we cannot see it, speak life into our dreams when they feel too heavy to carry, and anchor us in a sense of "we" when life makes us feel like an "I." In a society that so often demands Black women be endlessly self-reliant, friendship and sisterhood are radical acts of care, love, and survival.

PART ONE: Fall
Homecoming Season

Chapter One:

The Comfort of Sisterhood

When I think of fall, like many others in the HBCU (Historically Black Colleges and Universities) and Divine 9 families, my mind immediately goes to homecoming season. Homecoming is the ultimate family reunion. Alums—whether celebrating five, 25, or even 50-plus years since they last walked the yard as students—return from cities and towns across the world, all converging on one hallowed ground we call *home*.

I vividly remember Fisk University's sesquicentennial homecoming in 2016; not only because we were celebrating 150 years of our alma mater's legacy, but also because my undergraduate chapter of Zeta Phi Beta Sorority, Inc., was celebrating its 50th Charter Anniversary (shout out to Kappa Gamma!). There was a revival that took place within me once I spent time with my sorors, particularly amid the changing political tides that occurred on election night, just 12 hours before I had taken the Megabus to Nashville. I felt devastated by the results. Yet, what brought me back to life was the anticipation of being home. More than that, it was the embrace of my sister-friends and sorors that gave me peace and respite.

There is something profoundly reassuring about friendships where you can pick up right where you left off, even after years apart. That kind of bond reminds us that real love is never broken by time or distance. Gatherings like homecoming are communal practices that reaffirm identity and a sense of belonging. Each return reminds us that we are part of a lineage of strength, love, and shared experience. This continuity—tracing who we were as young women to who we are now—fortifies our sense of self across time. And you do not have to have lived life on an HBCU campus to know this feeling. Any act of returning— whether to your old neighborhood, your church, your hometown, or even to a friendship that has drifted—carries that same resonance.

In many ways, these reunions function as a form of collective therapy. The laughter, the storytelling, the simple act of showing up for one another—these are healing rituals. They give us space to release what we have been holding from the outside world while reconnecting with people who see us fully. People who truly know us. For Black women, friendships embody this dual role of memory and medicine. They remind us that, though the world changes and we ourselves change, the bonds of sisterhood can remain—enduring, steady, and restorative.

Mirror Moment (Write & Reflect): Think about a time when you returned to a place, community, or relationship that felt like home to you—whether physically or emotionally. What did that return reveal about who you are now compared to who you were then? How did the people, bonds, or traditions you reconnected with provide comfort, healing, or a sense of belonging?

_____

_____

_____

_____

_____

_____

_____

_____

_____

_____

_____

_____

_____

_____

_____

Girlfriend Gem Exercise: The Sisterhood Comfort List

Close your eyes and think of a time when being with your sister-friends brought you a deep sense of comfort. In the spaces below, finish this sentence: "I feel most at ease with my sisters when…" Examples might be: "…we laugh until our stomachs hurt," "…they remember little details about me," "…we sit in silence but still feel connected."

I feel most at ease with my sisters when:

_____

_____

I feel most at ease with my sisters when:

_____

_____

I feel most at ease with my sisters when:

_____

_____

Crown Check Affirmation:

I am never alone; the love of my sisters always finds me.

Soul Sista Soundtrack:

Swag Surfin' by F.L.Y.

Chapter 2:

Love Has *Everything* to Do With It

In setting the stage for why a study of love matters, bell hooks begins her seminal work *All About Love: New Visions* by reflecting on Tina Turner's anthem *What's Love Got to Do With It?* She identifies the song as emblematic of a cultural trend: a willingness to divest from love. The title itself suggests that love is everything but what it truly is. hooks challenges this idea, instead reminding us of an essential truth: love has *everything* to do with it.

This truth applies across all forms of relationships, including friendship. Yet for many of us, the idea of love within friendship has not always been familiar. As Dr. Thema Bryant points out in her book, *Matters of the Heart: Healing Your Relationship with Yourself and Those You Love*, too often, "love" is automatically confined to romance or to bonds between parent and child. This does not mean we fail to care for or show affection toward our friends—it simply means we have rarely been given permission to name that affection as love. Some of us even hesitate to tell our friends directly, "I love you."

Psychological research highlights the profound nature of this form of love. Attachment theory, which we will explore further in the next chapter, teaches us that secure and nurturing bonds—whether with parents, partners, or friends—are foundational to human well-being. Friendships, particularly those grounded in trust and reciprocity, offer emotional safety—and yet, friendship love is among the most healing and beautiful forms of love that often goes unrecognized. Love is—and should always be—the foundation of healthy friendship. Love shows up in how we are present for one another, in how we accept our friends without trying to alter the essence of who they are, and in how we honor the sacred space that allows both of us to grow tenderly and lovingly together.

Mirror Moment (Write & Reflect): When was the last time you told a friend, "I love you?" What feelings came up for you in that moment—ease, discomfort, hesitation, joy? What does that reveal about how you understand love within the context of friendship?

Girlfriend Gem Exercise: Friendship Constellation

In the center circle, write your name. In the larger circles around the center circle, write the names of friends who play a meaningful role in your life (you do not have to fill every circle). Next to each friend's name, write down one word or phrase that captures how they show you love (for example, "listens deeply," "challenges me," "makes me laugh," "shows up when I'm struggling"). Then, write one word or phrase about how you show love back to them.

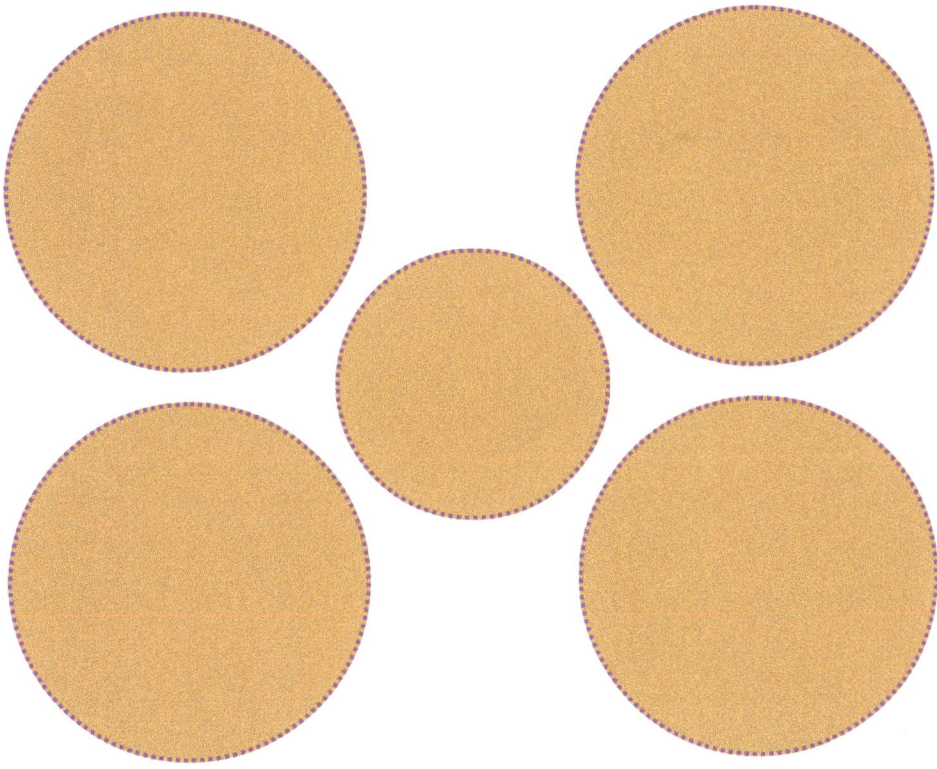

When you are finished, step back and look at your Friendship Constellation, and reflect on the following:

- What surprised you about your Friendship Constellation?
- Which friendships feel like safe spaces where you can speak and live freely?
- Where might you want to invest more intentional care?

Choose one friend from your Friendship Constellation and reach out to them this week with an act of intentional friendship love—whether that is saying "I love you," sending a note, or showing up concretely.

Crown Check Affirmation:

I honor the love I give and receive in my friendships. I am worthy of deep, healing, and sustaining love.

Soul Sista Soundtrack:

We Are Family by Sister Sledge

Chapter 3:

Attachment and Sisterhood

Attachment styles describe the ways we relate to others in close relationships, and they are largely shaped by our early interactions with our caregivers—primarily our parents. In the late 1950s and 1970s, through the work of John Bowlby and Mary Ainsworth, four traditional patterns of attachment were identified.

Secure Attachment is characterized as being comfortable with both intimacy and independence, trusting that others will be available when needed. *Anxious Attachment* is characterized by a longing for closeness and a fear of rejection or abandonment. *Avoidant Attachment* is characterized by high levels of independence and a tendency to withdraw from intimacy or emotional reliance. *Disorganized Attachment* is characterized by a tug-of-war between wanting closeness and resisting it.

More recent insight categorizes these patterns of attachment along two key dimensions: *attachment anxiety* (fear of being unloved, abandoned, or rejected) and *attachment avoidance* (a tendency to minimize emotional needs and maintain a distance from others). Secure attachment sits at the low end of both dimensions, while insecure attachment reflects different combinations of anxiety and avoidance.

In popular culture, attachment patterns are often discussed in the context of romantic relationships, but they also profoundly shape adult friendships—particularly how we trust, open up, resolve conflict, and respond to disappointment. For Black women, this dynamic is further layered by cultural context. Living within systems of racism, sexism, and historical betrayal, Black women frequently turn to one another for survival bonds that provide both affirmation and protection. It is precisely within our spaces of sisterhood that corrective attachment experiences often occur. Even if someone grew up with insecure attachment, friendships among Black women can re-teach safety, belonging, reciprocity, and trust.

Still, sisterhood can be both healing and exposing. The same relationships that nurture can also bring unhealed attachment wounds to the surface. This is why conscious reflection matters. Tending to our attachment patterns within the context of our friendships enables us to recognize our growth and the transformative power of the collective care provided by Black women.

For those of us navigating attachment anxiety, cultural pressures and stereotypes may intensify specific struggles, such as:

- *Fear of being "too much" or "too needy.* Dominant cultural narratives often dictate that Black women must be perpetually "strong," self-sufficient, and emotionally impenetrable. This makes it harder to voice needs without shame or fear of judgment.
- *Over-functioning in friendship.* Many Black women take on the role of the reliable caretaker—always showing up, helping, or sacrificing—even when it comes at significant personal cost. This pattern may be both a coping strategy and an internalized expectation.
- *Difficulty tolerating silence or space.* Because friendship often serves as a protective barrier against external hostility, distance from a close sister-friend may be experienced as abandonment rather than a natural rhythm in the relationship.
- *Jealousy or comparison.* Fear of being replaced or left out can arise when a friend grows close to others, threatening the sense of security in a bond that may already be carrying immense emotional weight.
- *People-pleasing.* To avoid rejection, we may suppress our own needs or boundaries, reinforcing cycles of self-neglect that echo broader societal devaluation.

For those of us navigating attachment avoidance, cultural pressures and stereotypes may intensify specific struggles, such as:

- *Hyper-independence as armor.* To protect against the possibility of rejection or disappointment, we may downplay or deny our own emotional needs, over-identifying with self-sufficiency in ways that align with cultural pressure to appear "unbothered" or "strong."
- *Discomfort with intimacy.* Deep emotional closeness in friendships can feel overwhelming or unsafe, leading to distancing behaviors such as withdrawing, minimizing problems, or keeping conversations superficial.
- *Reluctance to rely on others.* Even within supportive friendships, leaning on someone else can trigger feelings of guilt, shame, or fear of being perceived as a "burden," creating one-sided relational dynamics.
- *Quick exit strategies.* When conflict or misunderstanding arises, attachment avoidance may surface as cutting ties, ghosting, or creating distance rather than working through the discomfort of repair.
- *Suppressing emotional expression.* Feelings of sadness, fear, or disappointment may be withheld or rationalized away, reinforcing a cycle of invisibility and unmet needs.
- *Idealizing solitude.* Avoidance can masquerade as pride in "not needing anyone," which may offer short-term protection, but ultimately undermines the nourishment of deep connection.
- *Distrust of dependency.* Cultural narratives that equate dependence with weakness may amplify avoidance, making it harder to embrace interdependence as healthy.

Mirror Moment (Write & Reflect): How has sisterhood re-shaped the way you view closeness, trust, and relationship repair?

_____

_____

_____

_____

_____

_____

_____

_____

_____

_____

_____

_____

_____

_____

_____

_____

_____

How do you tend to move in your closest friendships? Answer honestly—this is about awareness, not judgment. Circle the response that feels most like you.

1. When a friend takes a while to respond to my text or call, I usually:

    a) Assume they are busy and we will reconnect soon.

    b) Worry if I did something wrong or if they are pulling away.

    c) Feel relieved—I like space and time to myself.

    d) Feel both anxious and distant—I want to reach out, but I also want to shut down.

2. When I am hurting, my first instinct is to:

    a) Reach out to a trusted friend and share what's on my heart.

    b) Hold it in until it feels "safe" to open up, afraid I will be judged or dismissed.

    c) Keep it to myself because I don't like depending on others.

    d) Bounce between wanting comfort and pushing people away.

3. In friendships, I often find myself:

    a) Giving and receiving love freely—I trust our bond.

    b) Being the one who over-functions (constantly checking in, helping, sacrificing).

    c) Pulling back when things get too emotional or vulnerable.

    d) Wanting closeness but not knowing how to handle it once I get it.

4. Silence or space in a friendship feels:

    a) Normal—bonds don't break just because of time apart.

    b) Uncomfortable—I worry it means I've been abandoned.

    c) Necessary—I feel smothered without enough space.

    d) Confusing—I crave closeness but also feel overwhelmed by it.

5. When a friend has other close relationships, I usually:
    a) Celebrate her connections and trust our bond is solid.
    b) Feel jealous or worried that I will be replaced.
    c) Feel detached—I do not really get jealous.
    d) Go back and forth—I want her closeness but also feel threatened.

6. My friendships teach me that:
    a) Love is steady, safe, and reciprocal.
    b) I have to prove my worth or risk being left behind.
    c) Relying on others is risky, so I depend on myself.
    d) Relationships are unpredictable—I never quite know what to expect.

7. When conflict arises with a close friend, I usually:
    a) Stay calm and talk it through with openness and respect.
    b) Feel panicked and try to fix it quickly so I do not lose her.
    c) Withdraw or avoid the conflict altogether.
    d) Feel torn—I want to resolve it, but also want to shut down.

8. When my friend celebrates a success, I typically feel:
    a) Genuinely happy and supportive—I love seeing her shine.
    b) Happy for her, but also secretly worried I will fall behind or be forgotten.
    c) Neutral—it does not affect me much either way.
    d) Both proud of her and insecure about my own place in the friendship.

9. If I sense a shift in the friendship (fewer texts, less time together), I usually:
    a) Trust that our connection is still strong.
    b) Feel anxious and want to "chase" closeness.
    c) Detach and convince myself I don't need her.
    d) Swing between wanting more reassurance and wanting to retreat.

10. When a friend shows me deep love or affection, I tend to:
  a) Receive it with gratitude—it feels natural and safe.
  b) Feel nervous, wondering if I can keep it.
  c) Feel uncomfortable or pull back from the intensity.
  d) Want it badly, but doubt if I deserve it.

11. If I am going through a significant life change, I usually:
  a) Lean on my friends, knowing they will be there.
  b) Worry they will not want to deal with my "mess."
  c) Handle it on my own and avoid burdening anyone.
  d) Crave their support but push them away at the same time.

12. The way I usually experience closeness in friendships is:
  a) Warm, consistent, and easy to trust.
  b) Full of highs and lows—I feel deeply connected, then fearful of losing it.
  c) A bit distant—I like connection, but only to a certain point.
  d) Confusing—I want intimacy, but I struggle to feel settled in it.

Scoring: Your score will reveal your tendency towards one of the four attachment styles. It is important to remember that attachment styles are not permanent. They can change based on our immediate environment, circumstances, and our personal willingness toward growth. Consider revisiting this quiz after some time has passed, and you have actively engaged in your own personal healing journey, to see your growth or varied tendencies over time.

Mostly A's: Secure Attachment You are comfortable with closeness and independence. You trust that bonds can handle space, silence, and change.

Mostly B's: Anxious Attachment You crave closeness but often worry about being "too much" or being abandoned. You may over-give to keep relationships strong.

Mostly C's: Avoidant Attachment

You value independence and may struggle to fully let people in. You protect your heart by staying self-reliant, which can sometimes lead to feelings of resentment towards your friends.

Mostly D's: Disorganized Attachment

You desire intimacy but also fear it. This push-pull can make relationships feel complicated and intense, often tied to earlier trauma.

Crown Check Affirmation:

My needs are not a burden, and my love is not too much. I am worthy of friendships that honor both my strength and my softness. I release the old fears that shaped how I connect, and I welcome bonds that are steady, reciprocal, and healing.

Soul Sista Soundtrack:

What About Your Friends by TLC

Chapter 4:

When Life Paths Shift

For many of us, there may come a time when the women we laughed with every weekend start texting back with "let me check my calendar." The time between calls stretches out. The inside jokes grow faint. Suddenly, one friend is deep in diapers and daycare drama, another is planning solo trips on some tropical island, and yet another is swamped with back-to-back business launches. Life does not always keep our timelines in sync, and that can create a quiet distance we do not always know how to name.

Some of us are single and figuring out who we are. Some of us are married with children and figuring out how to not lose ourselves. Some are caretakers, exhausted and stretched to the limit. Others are finally making time for rest. The rhythms of our lives shift, and with them, the rhythm of our friendships does, too. These changes may sometimes be misinterpreted as neglect, distance, or disinterest, when, in fact, they might reflect changing responsibilities and priorities—not a change in love.

There is sometimes an unspoken belief that "real" friends do not need to explain themselves—that loyalty should survive any storm, big or small. The truth is that we are all doing the best we can in different seasons, and sometimes that "best" looks like needing more space, more understanding, or even more communication than we initially expected.

Secure relationships are built on a foundation of trusting that the connection can bend without breaking. When we understand that our closeness may ebb and flow with the demands of life, we allow ourselves, and others, more grace. What matters most is not constant proximity, but the sense of emotional safety—that "you are still there for me, even if we do not talk every day."

This is not to say that we let these ebbs silently destroy our otherwise healthy friendships. Even through the shifts in seasons, healthy friendships still require open and honest communication. In adulthood, friendship requires more intentionality. We no longer have the seemingly unlimited access we once had, living in dorms on our college campuses, attending parties, or hanging out at the nail shop as consistently as we did before our roles and responsibilities changed. Now, we might bump into each other at community events, the grocery store, the salon, or we might see each other every Sunday at church. Showing up becomes more of a choice and less of a convenience.

We know that adult bonds thrive on responsiveness, accessibility, and emotional engagement. That does not have to mean daily contact—it can look like:

- A thoughtful check-in text once a week.
- A monthly FaceTime call.
- A shared meme that says, "This made me think of you."
- A message that says, "I miss you. I want to schedule a sister-friend date. Here are the days and times that work for me. What days and times work for you?"

For some of us, this kind of planned connection might feel unnatural or even performative—but it is not. It is simply adapting to a new rhythm of care. We are learning to navigate the seasons of life, recognizing how our roles and needs evolve, and staying emotionally available to those we care about in ways that feel manageable and meaningful. Intentionality does not dilute the bond—it honors it.

Mirror Moment (Write & Reflect): What phase of life are you in right now—emotionally, physically, spiritually? How has that shaped how you show up in friendship?

_____

_____

_____

_____

_____

_____

_____

_____

_____

_____

_____

_____

_____

_____

_____

_____

_____

Girlfriend Gem Exercise: Friendship Capacity

Inside each section—Time, Energy, Emotional Support, and Availability—write a short description of what you currently have to give. Then ask yourself: What would it look like to communicate this honestly to a friend—without guilt or apology?

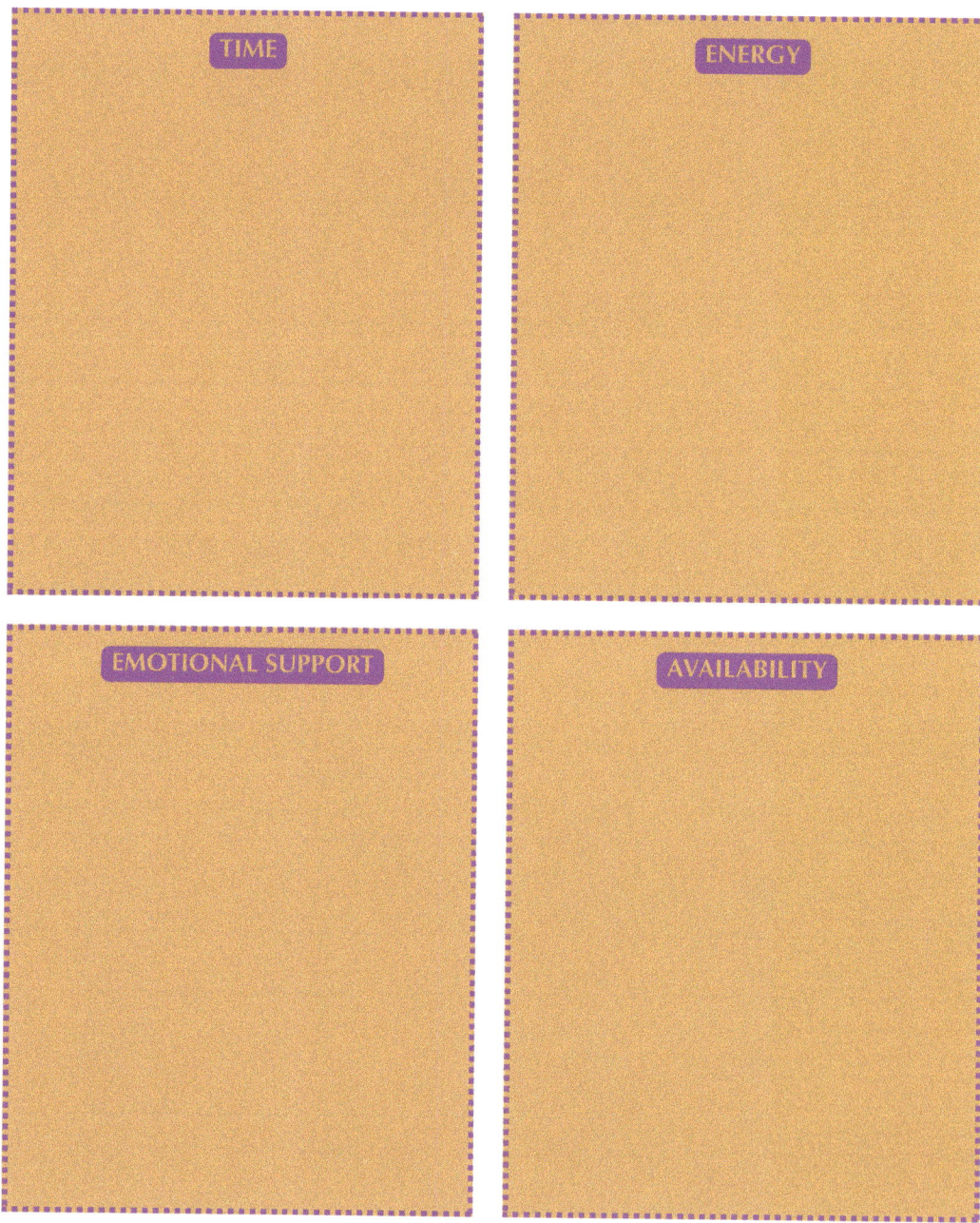

Sister Scenario: Shanice became a new mom and found herself too exhausted to keep up with her usual outings with her friend group. Her best friend Erica felt abandoned and told others, "Shanice forgot about us since she had that baby."

Reflection Questions:

1. What could Erica have done to voice her needs?
2. How can Shanice honor her limitations while still showing care and consideration?

Practice:

Offer each other grace in new seasons. Ask: "How can I show up for you now, in a way that fits this season?"

Crown Check Affirmation:

Our paths can part and still run parallel in love. My friendships don't have to look like they used to, to still be genuine. We grow. We shift. We evolve.

Soul Sista Soundtrack:

Count on Me by
Whitney Houston & CeCe Winans

Chapter 5:

I Am Changing: Values, Beliefs, and Becoming Ourselves

Have you ever come home—whether from college, a big move, or just a season of growth—and met up with an old friend, only to realize… "Yeah, we just do not vibe the same anymore?" It is not necessarily that they have changed in a bad way. In fact, they may still be the same silly, fun, adventurous, carefree person you have always known. But that is just it—they have not changed. Or at least, not in the direction of growth that you have been moving toward. Perhaps they no longer see the world the way you do. Maybe you no longer see it the way you both once did. That realization can feel jarring. In some cases, it could become a threat to the friendship—especially when deeply held values, beliefs, or political views start to surface and collide. Evolving beliefs, such as faith, can feel like betrayal within tight-knit communities.

In the memorable opening line from the television series *Insecure*, Season 4, Episode 5, "Lowkey Movin' On," where Issa is talking to her brother on the phone, she says, "I don't really f*** with Molly anymore." Issa says this after a series of awkward encounters with her college best friend, Molly; but if we take a closer look underneath the layers, both Issa and Molly were growing in different ways, in their own right. This is not a bad thing, nor is it inherently detrimental to a friendship. What was crucial for them, and for many of us, was learning how to grow together without it involving arguing. We can learn to speak truth to what is occurring between us—after all, she is our sis.

Some friendships can weather these kinds of growing pains; others cannot. While that is hard to accept, it is also OK. We get to choose how we move forward. We get to redefine connection. If the bond fades, there does not have to be love lost. Growth does not always mean holding on. Sometimes it means letting go, with grace.

Value divergence is one of the most common sources of strain in adult relationships, particularly in friendships formed during earlier, more identity-fluid stages of life. Value divergence occurs when two people start to hold different beliefs or prioritize other aspects of life. As we mature, our values often become more clearly defined through lived experience, introspection, and social context. When our values begin to diverge from those of long-time friends, tension can arise—not necessarily because of hostility, but because the shared framework that once bonded us begins to look different.

Social learning theory suggests that much of our behavior and belief formation is shaped through observation, modeling, and reinforcement within our environment. So when we encounter someone—especially someone we have known for years—whose values seem "stuck" or misaligned, it can feel unsettling. What we might really be noticing is a misalignment in the environments we have been exposed to, the beliefs we have internalized, and the ways we have been shaped by reinforcement over time. In essence, we have learned different things, and those learnings are now producing tension.

This is where intentional curiosity becomes crucial. Value divergence does not have to signal the end of a friendship. It can become an opportunity to explore different worldviews if approached with an open mind rather than judgment. That said, this kind of curiosity takes work—and for many, it can feel counterintuitive, especially since our brains are wired for safety and a sense of belonging. Exploring beliefs that oppose our own can feel like a personal threat; particularly when those beliefs challenge our core identities or the realities we live in.

Each person is living out a unique story shaped by culture, family, trauma, community, and personal meaning. Understanding the values of others means trying to understand their story, not just debating their stance. It is essential to hold this nuance; respecting the values of others does not require you to adopt them as your own. Coexistence is possible—and often necessary—to a degree. Additionally, if a person has values that actively endanger your physical, emotional, or psychological well-being—if their beliefs uphold systems of racism, sexism, homophobia, or other forms of oppression—then distancing yourself, or ending the relationship may become a necessary boundary you create, and that is OK. Boundaries are not a betrayal of empathy; they are an expression of self-respect.

In short: value divergence is not inherently a crisis; it can be an invitation to reflect. Curiosity is a skill, and safety—yours and the safety of others—is always the baseline for connection.

Mirror Moment (Write & Reflect): What values and beliefs do you hold close that you want to keep? Which ones are you willing to explore beyond, and how does this impact your friendships?

_____

_____

_____

_____

_____

_____

_____

_____

_____

_____

_____

_____

Girlfriend Gem Exercise: Beliefs Bubbles

Consider a friend with whom you are noticing a slight divergence in values. Map out where you align, and where you differ. Then, reflect: what does this reveal about you, your friend(s), and your friendship(s)? How do these revelations impact your friendship(s)?

YOU   **BOTH**   **YOUR FRIEND**

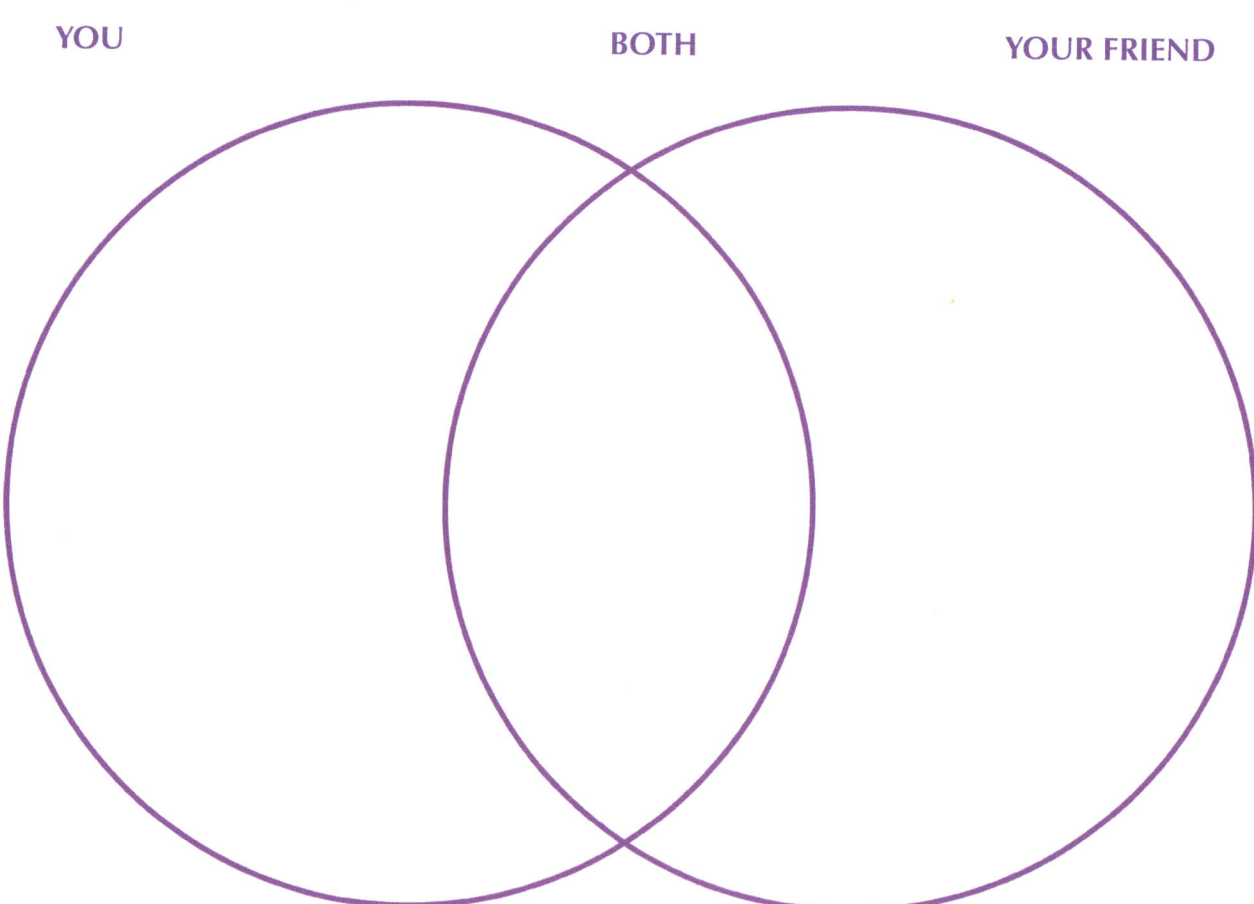

Crown Check Affirmation:

I can change and still be cherished.
They can change, and still be loved,
even if from a distance.

Soul Sista Soundtrack:

U.N.I.T.Y. by Queen Latifah

PART TWO: Winter
The Coldest Sister Ever

Chapter 6:

Emotional Labor, Burnout, and Being the Strong Friend

The "strong Black woman" archetype does not just shape how we present ourselves at work or in our families—it also influences our friendships. If we are not careful, it can silence the signs of burnout and mask over-functioning. It teaches us, often subconsciously, to prioritize being needed over being nurtured.

If you are the friend everyone turns to—all the time, for everything—the deeper question becomes: who shows up for you? Your needs matter just as much. If your friendship feels like it is built solely on how much you can give—without space to set boundaries, take breaks, or say no—that is not true friendship. That may be a sign of emotional manipulation, which is not characteristic of healthy, reciprocal relationships.

Sometimes, we mimic what we have seen modeled by the people in our immediate environment. Perhaps we grew up watching the women in our families maintain one-sided friendships. Maybe we were taught that being "a good friend" meant being endlessly available, even at our own expense.

I watched my mother embody the principles of mutuality and reciprocity in her friendships. She gave love freely, but she received it, too. She went to their homes, and they came to ours. She celebrated with them, and they celebrated with her. She mourned with them, and they mourned with her. This is part of what has defined sisterhood in my own life.

While her friendships were mostly positive models for me, not every one of them lasted. When some relationships fell away, it was often because boundaries were crossed repeatedly—with no willingness to change. My mother knew how to hold love and limits at the same time. She taught me that real friendship is about showing up for each other—but not to the point of burnout.

Emotional labor imbalance is a common cause of friendship fatigue, resentment, and disconnection. When one person consistently bears the emotional weight of the friendship—doing the checking in, the caregiving, and the supporting—while the others remain emotionally unavailable or disengaged, the dynamic becomes unsustainable. Over time, it can leave even the most caring friend feeling invisible, depleted, and alone.

Returning to the theory of attachment, understanding our own attachment styles can help us better comprehend what is truly happening—not just in the friendship, but within ourselves. For some of us, early attachments may have been marked by avoidance or emotional neglect, leading to a deep discomfort with vulnerability. This often shows up as hyper-independence in adult friendships—the tendency to withdraw, avoid asking for help, or carry everything alone. These are the friends who say, "It is fine, I will just do it myself," even when they are overwhelmed. Often labeled as "the strong friend," they may be deeply trusted but rarely truly known.

Mirror Moment (Write & Reflect): What stands in the way of you asking for support, even when it is necessary?

_____

_____

_____

_____

_____

_____

_____

_____

_____

_____

_____

_____

_____

Girlfriend Gem Exercise: Reaching Resentment Thermometer

Sis… are you over-giving? Review the checklist below and check all that resonate with you presently regarding your friendships. When you are done, tally up the number of items you checked on the list. Use the rubric below to see where you land on the Reaching Resentment Thermometer.

- [ ] Frequent frustration over small things related to your friend(s).
- [ ] Irritability toward a friend or situation that used to feel neutral.
- [ ] Bitterness when thinking about past interactions with a friend.
- [ ] Feeling unappreciated or taken for granted.
- [ ] Loss of compassion for the other person's struggles.

- [ ] Avoiding communication or withdrawing from interactions.
- [ ] Passive-aggressive comments or sarcasm slipping into conversations.
- [ ] Keeping score of favors, wrongs, or unmet expectations.
- [ ] Withholding effort (not helping, contributing, or engaging fully).
- [ ] Replaying arguments in your head instead of letting them go.
- [ ] Fantasizing about "teaching them a lesson."
- [ ] Assuming bad intentions behind their actions, even when unclear.
- [ ] Fixating on fairness and comparing what you give vs. what you get.
- [ ] Feeling stuck, as if nothing will change, and simmering in silence.
- [ ] Interpreting neutral actions as criticism or disrespect.
- [ ] Tension in your body (jaw clenching, tight shoulders) when around them.
- [ ] Less patience, snapping quickly at them.
- [ ] Emotional distancing—affection, warmth, or trust fades.
- [ ] Loss of joy in shared activities that once felt enjoyable.
- [ ] Thinking of leaving the friendship rather than addressing the issue.

1–5 Points: Spring — Awareness Blossoms (Early Awareness Zone)

You are noticing little irritations budding. This is a sign to pause, water yourself with reflection, and plant boundaries early. With care, these small tensions do not have to grow into weeds.

6–10 Points: Summer — Heat Rising (Warning Zone)

The warmth between sisters is still there, but the heat of frustration is building. You may feel drained or quick to pull back. This is a sign to speak truth with love, lean into honesty, and protect your energy so the bond can thrive under the sun.

11–15 Points: Autumn — Leaves Turning (Critical Zone)

Things are shifting. You may be replaying old hurts, keeping score, or seeing the connection lose its color. This is the season to shed what no longer serves you, or the friendship. Honest conversations and intentional boundaries are needed for renewal.

16–20 Points: Winter — Heart on Freeze (Overload Zone)

The bond feels cold, compassion has thinned, and joy is buried beneath resentment. This is a signal for reckoning. It may require deep rest, courageous dialogue, or even releasing the connection. Winter asks you to decide: will you restore the soil for new growth, or let this chapter close?

Crown Check Affirmation:

I am allowed to rest in my friendships. My rest is not abandonment. It preserves the friendships that truly matter.

Soul Sista Soundtrack:

Girl by Destiny's Child

Chapter 7:

The Four Manifestations of Friendship Wounds

I think of friendship wounds as having four primary forms of manifestation:

Body: physical symptoms and behaviors.
Heart: emotions of grief, anger, sadness, longing, etc.
Ego: identity and self-concept are bruised.
Soul: spiritual loss, and an altered essence.

The body is where the wound manifests physically, manifesting as tight shoulders, a heavy chest, restless sleep, loss of appetite, and even fatigue. The body often bears the scars of friendship before the mind fully names them. The heart holds the memories of closeness, intimacy, and the ache of absence. It is not about identity (ego) or essence (soul), but about the immediate tenderness of emotions that swell and recede with time. The ego represents feelings of jealousy, envy, comparison, and even defensiveness as a form of trying to protect the damaged ego. The soul represents resentment and bitterness. This layer shows up as questioning our self-worth, and might manifest as the belief that "I am (or she is) not worthy of friendship," or "I am (or she is) not lovable."

Some friendship wounds, if properly tended to, can be resolved. However, as we delve deeper, it can become increasingly challenging—not impossible—to overcome the pain. We will discuss healing friendship wounds in more depth in later chapters.

Friendship wounds often cut deep because friendships are usually where we feel most seen as our everyday selves. Unlike romantic relationships or family ties, friendships frequently grow without formal commitments. Healing begins by making space for these painful emotions rather than trying to push them away. Instead of telling yourself you shouldn't feel hurt or rushing to get over it, it is essential to acknowledge the sadness, anger, or loneliness without judgment—much like sitting beside a guest who comes to visit. This practice of acceptance acknowledges that grief is part of love.

It is also helpful to take a step back from self-critical thoughts that may arise, like "I was not a good enough friend" or "I am unlovable." By observing these thoughts instead of getting caught up in them, we create space to remember that our worth is not determined by one relationship.

By doing so, we kick-start a return to our values—the kind of friend, sister, or woman we still want to be, even in the face of strained friendships. The wound may remind us that we value loyalty, joy, or reciprocity, and those values can guide how we nurture existing friendships or open ourselves to new ones. In this way, friendship wounds do not just mark an ending; they may invite us into a process of living more fully and intentionally, carrying forward the lessons of what matters most in our connections.

● ● ● ● ● ● ● ● ● ● ● ● ● ● ●

Mirror Moment (Write & Reflect): Bring to mind a sister-friend with whom you were once close. Based on the Four Manifestations of Friendship Wounds, identify where the wound manifested itself. In a timeline format, map out your "Friendship Timeline" to identify how and when things changed. This is not meant to place blame, but to take an accurate assessment and hold yourself accountable for your own patterns and behaviors in the friendship, and to identify what you might have done differently if given the opportunity.

_____

_____

_____

_____

_____

_____

_____

_____

_____

_____

_____

_____

_____

_____

_____

_____

_____

Girlfriend Gem Exercise: Mindful Friendship Meditation: Moving Through Friendship Wounds

Notice Your Experience. Find a quiet space to sit alone, or with a group of trusted friends. Pause, breathe, and recall a recent moment of tension, distance, or hurt in a friendship. Notice the thoughts that arose, the emotions you felt, and where they live in your body.

Practice Acceptance. Allow those feelings to be present without judgment. Remind yourself: "It is OK to feel this way. These feelings are part of my experience, but they do not define me."

Defuse from Thoughts. Picture your thoughts as clouds or leaves drifting by. You do not need to hold onto them or believe everything they say. Gently remind yourself: "These are just thoughts, not facts."

Reconnect with Values. Ask yourself: What kind of friend do I want to be, even when friendship feels painful or uncertain? What values guide how I show up in my relationships?

Sister Scenario: During a heated, offline conversation, Maya told Brianna that she hurt her feelings. Brianna responded defensively, and later that evening, she left the group chat and blocked Maya on social media. The friendship ended without any closure.

Reflection Questions:

1. What does "ghosting" communicate in friendships?
2. How might Maya carry this wound into future relationships?
3. What healthier conflict responses could Brianna have tried?

Practice:

Instead of vanishing, take space and name it: "I need a pause, but I value this friendship. Let's talk when I'm calmer."

Crown Check Affirmation:

My feelings deserve space. I tend to my friendship wounds with love and care.

Soul Sista Soundtrack:

Special by LIZZO

Chapter 8:

Identifying the Source of the Pain:
Betrayal, Competition, and Insecurity in Sisterhood

Based on both lived and professional experience, three of the most common threats that lead to wounds in friendships are betrayal, competition, and insecurity. These wounds manifest in various ways, but they share a common thread: they disrupt trust and connection, often leaving deep emotional scars.

Betrayal can manifest as stealing, lying, or crossing boundaries with a friend or loved one. It may also appear in more subtle ways, such as sharing a secret thoughtlessly rather than maliciously. While the motives behind the more subtle forms of betrayal may stem from fear, immaturity, or survival strategies (rather than cruelty), the impact is still painful. Betrayal, no matter the motive, erodes trust and makes vulnerability feel unsafe.

Competition in friendships can be a slow burn. Sometimes, friends may measure themselves against each other's achievements, relationships, or even style. This can come from a craving for belonging or recognition, and in some cases, proximity—wanting to be close enough to observe, imitate, or even "one up" a friend. Within Black women's friendships, colorism, misogynoir, and "mean girl" culture can add another painful layer, where Eurocentric standards of beauty and lifestyle create a hierarchy that fuels unspoken rivalries and undermines solidarity. *Colorism* is discrimination based on skin-tone, where lighter skin is privileged over darker skin. It often occurs within the same racial or ethnic group and influences social and econonomic opportunities. *Misogynoir* is a form of discrimination that specifically targets Black women, combining racism and sexism. It describes the unique stereotypes, bias, and mistreatment directed at Black women because we are both Black and female.

At the root of much competition often lies insecurity and jealousy. Jealousy tends to be outward-facing, such as fearing replacement, abandonment, or being left behind when a friend enters a new stage of life. Insecurity tends to be more inward-facing, rooted in self-doubt and questions of worthiness. Insecurity is often the soil where jealousy takes root; without it, jealousy may be fleeting, but with it, jealousy can grow into chronic tension. Recognizing these dynamics does not erase the pain they cause. However, it does help us understand that they sometimes spring from unmet needs and unhealed wounds, rather than a lack of love.

Past wounds from adolescence or systemic trauma can quietly shape the way we experience and navigate friendships as adults. Suppose early relationships were marked by rejection, betrayal, or the subtle sting of being overlooked. In that case, those memories can prime us to expect similar dynamics in our present connections. Systemic trauma—whether through racism, sexism, or class barriers—adds another layer, fostering mistrust or comparison that makes vulnerability difficult. For some of us, the friendships we form later in life are unconsciously filtered through the lens of these old injuries, leaving us either hyper-vigilant to signs of exclusion or overly self-critical in the face of perceived differences.

Cultural insight deepens this picture, as internalized white supremacy, desirability bias (the tendency to favor people or traits deemed socially attractive, leading to unequal attention, opportunities or treatment), and classism often play out beneath the surface of friendships. These forces can distort how we measure our worth in comparison to others, privileging proximity to whiteness, beauty standards, or wealth in ways that erode authentic connection. Unresolved dynamics of colorism, sibling rivalry, and the expectation to embody the "strong Black woman" archetype can heighten the sting of conflict or distance between friends. What may appear to be a simple misunderstanding can carry the weight of complex histories, amplifying the pain of friendship wounds.

The work of healing, then, involves spotting the relational patterns we unconsciously repeat. Do you find yourself withdrawing at the first hint of rejection? Over-giving in hopes of securing belonging? Competing silently with those you love? Recognizing these cycles allows you to interrupt them before they harden into self-fulfilling prophecies. By identifying how past wounds resurface in the present, you create space for friendships that honor your full humanity, free from scripts written by trauma and systemic bias.

Mirror Moment (Write & Reflect): What past wounds still speak to you/for you in the present? Who do you feel "less than" around, and why?

_____

_____

_____

_____

_____

_____

_____

_____

_____

_____

_____

_____

_____

_____

_____

Girlfriend Gem Exercise: Friendship Pattern Tracker

Friendship History: List 3–5 of your most significant friendships (past or present). For each one, write: What drew me to this friend at first? What role did I often play in this friendship (supporter, competitor, nurturer, listener, leader, etc.)? What role did they often play? How has the friendship shifted (if it did)?

_____

_____

_____

_____

_____

_____

_____

_____

_____

_____

_____

_____

_____

_____

_____

_____

Spotting Patterns: Put a check next to the common threads across your friendships:

Ask yourself: Do I tend to choose friends who...

- ☐ Struggle with jealousy/competition?
- ☐ Lean on me as the "strong one?"
- ☐ Mirror my insecurities back to me?
- ☐ Make me feel like I have to prove my worth?
- ☐ Push me toward growth and accountability?

Ask yourself: How do I usually show up?

- ☐ Do I over-give to earn loyalty?
- ☐ Do I struggle to express my needs?
- ☐ Do I withdraw when I feel vulnerable or betrayed?

Cultural Insight Check-In: Reflect on how cultural dynamics may shape your patterns. Ask yourself: Have I felt pressure to be the "strong Black woman" in my friendships? Has colorism, desirability bias, or classism played a role in who I am drawn to—or who is drawn to me? Do I sometimes confuse loyalty with silence about harm? How do systemic wounds (racism, sexism, generational trauma) show up in my friendships?

_____

_____

_____

_____

_____

_____

_____

_____

_____

_____

_____

_____

_____

_____

_____

_____

_____

_____

Red Flags & Green Flags: In the Red Flags column, list some early signs that you might be repeating unhealthy patterns (for example, feeling like you cannot be vulnerable, constant comparisons, unspoken needs). In the Green Flags column, list signs you might be building healthier friendships (for example, mutual care, honesty without fear, space for joy and vulnerability, accountability without shame).

RED FLAGS	GREEN FLAGS

New Intentions: In the space provided, write one pattern you want to release, one quality you want to invite into your friendships, and one boundary or practice you will honor moving forward.

Pattern:

_____

_____

Quality:

_____

_____

Boundary:

_____

_____

Sister Scenario: Jasmine confided in her friend Simone about her struggles in her marriage. Weeks later, Jasmine learned Simone shared the details with their mutual friends, saying, "I was just worried about her, that's why I told them."

Reflection Questions:
1. What lines did Simone cross, even if her intent was concern?
2. How might "concern" become a cover for gossip?
3. What conversations are needed to repair this situation?

Practice:
Before sharing another woman's story, ask: Would I say this if she were standing here? For repair: an honest apology with changed behavior—not excuses—is required.

Crown Check Affirmation:

There is space for all of us to shine.

Soul Sista Soundtrack:

Carbon Copy by Choklate

PART THREE: Spring
No Shade, Just Growth

Chapter 9:

Coexisting in Spaces and Circles When Ruptures Occur

When ruptures occur in friendships and reconciliation has not been achieved, it can be challenging to share the same spaces with people we no longer communicate with. Whether it is at work, church, or in organizations, navigating environments with someone we have had a falling out with can feel brutal. On top of that, social media can intensify the sting—seeing photos of gatherings or celebrations can trigger FOMO (fear of missing out) and spark thoughts that do not always reflect reality.

In these moments, cognitive distortions, or irrational thinking patterns that skew how we interpret situations and reinforce negative emotions or beliefs, often creep in, especially with "silent beefs" where the root of the tension is unclear. We may start assuming, for example, "They did not invite me because they are mad," or "They do not want me around anymore." These assumptions are sometimes fueled by fear or insecurity rather than evidence. This kind of ambiguous loss—grieving someone who is still alive—is real and valid.

Part of coping with this loss is developing emotional awareness. Most of us can quickly identify happiness, sadness, anger, or fear, but friendships often evoke complex and layered emotions. Suspicion may mask fear of losing someone we love, while curiosity, disbelief, or even anger might surface alongside it. Mixed emotions can be confusing, especially when past trauma makes them harder to untangle.

The key is to pause and name what you are feeling with honesty and compassion. Treat emotions as signals rather than absolute truths, and approach them with curiosity before accepting them as fact. This helps us stay grounded, even when distortions or anxieties cloud our interpretations, and opens the door to more intentional healing. Thoughts are mental events, not facts. It is essential to acknowledge these distortions without succumbing to them, to recognize when we are caught in the grip of unhelpful narratives, and to gently redirect our focus back to what truly matters.

FOMO can become an obsession that steals our attention and energy. It can pull us away from nurturing the very friendships that sustain us in real life. The more we fixate on what we are missing, the less we invest in presence and cultivating connections to meet our friendship needs. This can deepen feelings of isolation, sadness, and anxiety, and lead us into harmful cycles of comparison—comparing our complicated lives to the polished highlights others share online. By practicing mindfulness and staying rooted in our values, we can reclaim our power from the swirling noise of FOMO and social media. We remind ourselves that the heart of sisterhood beats strongest in real moments of care, not in the filtered frames of online life.

Additionally, I think it is important to remind us that if remaining in these shared spaces and circles is just too painful for us while navigating our friendship wounds, it is OK to set boundaries, or even take breaks from the shared spaces if necessary. Now, if you both work in the same office, that might be a bit challenging—but not impossible. I am not suggesting that you quit your job if you are beefin' with your work bestie, or that you end your membership in your mutual organization. What I am recommending is that you take intentional action to ensure the shared environment carries as minimal tension as possible.

This might look like:
- Respectfully, yet firmly, redirecting anyone who asks questions or makes comments about the observed change in dynamic between you and your friend(s). You might say, "Respectfully, I do not want to talk about that right now," or "She and I are not com-

municating right now, so I do not feel comfortable speaking to you about her/this." If the person keeps pressing, you can resist the urge to overshare. We are not obligated to speak on our friendship wounds with anyone who is not a safe person to us.

- If it is a shared organization, church, or space like a gym, it might be necessary to take a short break. Maybe skip a meeting, attend virtually if hybrid attendance is offered, or take a Sunday to attend virtual church service. There is no shame in taking a break to tend to our hearts.

- If the mutual space is the work environment, instead of eating lunch in your typical meetup spot, you can choose another area to have lunch. If you're able, you could use your lunch break to eat out and do some quick errands, read a book, take a walk, or listen to some music.

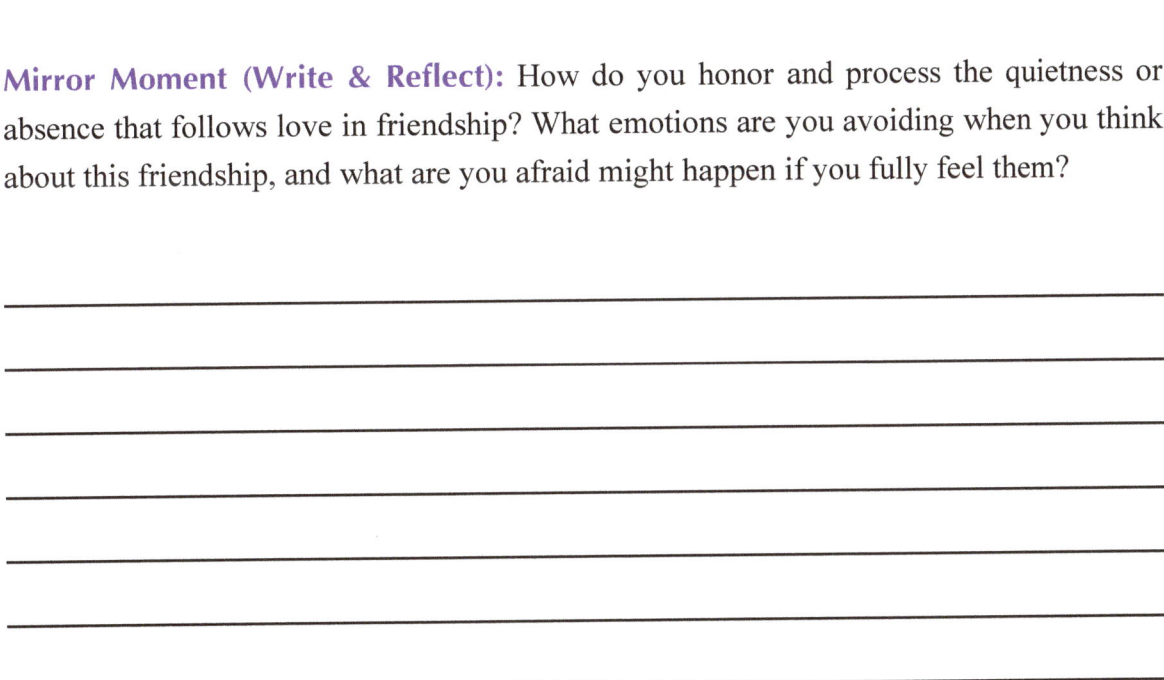

Mirror Moment (Write & Reflect): How do you honor and process the quietness or absence that follows love in friendship? What emotions are you avoiding when you think about this friendship, and what are you afraid might happen if you fully feel them?

_____

_____

_____

_____

_____

_____

_____

Girlfriend Gem Exercise: Who Is In Your Circle

Each ripple in the concentric circles below represents levels of closeness, trust, or frequency of interaction. The center represents you. The inner circle represents the deep, intimate, soul-level friends (those you can call at 3:00 a.m.). The middle circle represents strong but not constant friendships (you share joy and trust, but not daily intimacy). The outer circle represents acquaintances, casual friends, or situational connections (such as work, community groups, or social media). Add friends, sisters, aunts, community members, or mentors to the rings that best represent your relationship/connection with them.

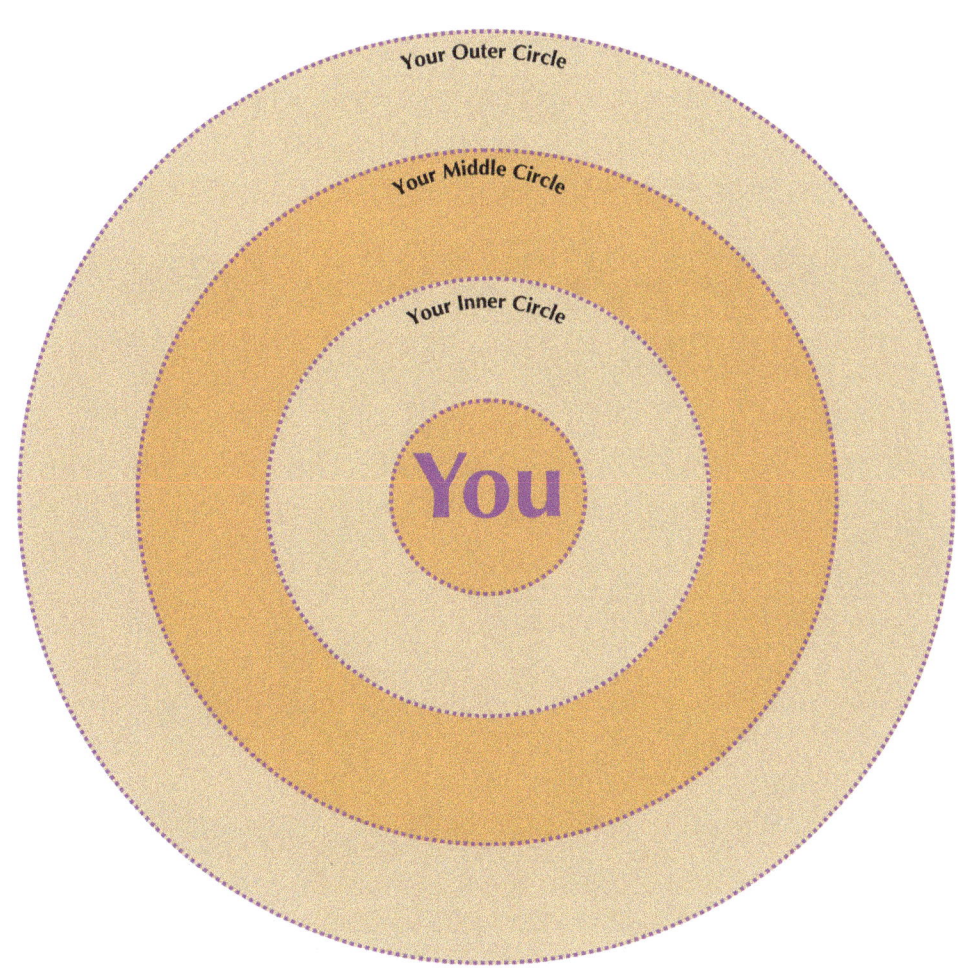

After filling in the circles, reflect on the following:

Which friendships bring me joy, laughter, or healing?
Which ones feel heavy, one-sided, or draining?
Who respects my boundaries and affirms my growth?
How has my circle changed in the last year?
Who has moved inward, outward, or away altogether—and how do I feel about that?
Who do I want to grow closer to?

You can create a new set of circles every season (or on your birthday, or at the New Year) to track how your friendships evolve over time. Over months or years, this becomes a visual record of your changing friendship landscape and your own growth, as well as any challenging areas you encounter while navigating it.

Crown Check Affirmation:

My worth is not defined by who tags me or texts me back. I am allowed to take up space. And they are, too.

Soul Sista Soundtrack:

FOMO by Amber Mark

Chapter 10:

Addressing Conflict and Deciding to Remain or Release

Many factors contribute to the weight of the challenging decisions we face in wintry friendship seasons, particularly in two key areas: first, whether to address conflict with our friends, and second, what to do once we have addressed the conflict—whether to rebuild or end the friendship. Many of us do not have the language to name what we are experiencing mentally and emotionally when we are wounded in any of our relationships, particularly our friendships. Instead, we are often left with silence, assumptions, and stories we tell ourselves. Sometimes, we overlook the importance of pausing to investigate and to consider context. Or we do not react at all. We sit quietly in the distance. We swallow the ache. We let the gap widen—not from lack of love, but from lack of knowing what to do with the in-between.

Healing spaces require new scripts. What if we gave each other permission to ask, "Are we good?" What if we could say, "I noticed some distance—can we talk about it?" without assuming the worst or fearing that we will lose face? In doing so, we begin to re-write the narrative—one where strength and softness can coexist. One where silence does not become the final word.

There appears to be an unspoken belief we have collectively inherited—often shaped by survival, cultural expectations, and generational messages—that reaching out first makes you weak. We assume that initiating repair means you are "the problem." Checking in, clarifying, or saying "I miss you" is somehow perceived as being thirsty, "pressured," or inviting drama. That is not the truth. The truth is that reaching out is an act of courage. It requires emotional maturity. It says, "This relationship matters to me. I just want to understand what happened."

Additionally, many of us were taught to be strong, self-sufficient, and emotionally guarded. Vulnerability was not always modeled for us—it was often dismissed as unsafe or unnecessary. So when friendships start to drift, silence becomes our default.

This is why the decision to rebuild or to release a friendship requires deep intentionality. It requires us to check in with ourselves, and ask:

- If nothing changed, could I still accept this person as they are?
- Do I feel emotionally safe enough to be honest with them?
- What decision best honors my peace, my values, and my growth?
- What are my expectations of this friendship?
- What do I truly desire here—clarity, repair, or closure?
- Do I have the capacity to keep showing up in this connection as it is?

Sometimes a friendship is simply in a winter season, where distance is protective but spring will return. Other times, the leaves have already fallen, signaling the natural end of its life cycle. Wisdom lies in discerning the difference.

Consider leaning in to rebuild a friendship with your sister-friend if:
- The friendship has real value to you. You miss their presence, and the relationship has brought more joy than harm.
- The shift feels unclear. Something happened, but you do not fully understand why the energy changed. A conversation could bring clarity.
- There has been a misunderstanding. Minor miscommunications or unspoken assumptions may be at the root of the drift.

- The friendship feels worth the effort. Even if it is uncomfortable, you sense that healing or reconnection is possible.
- You still trust their character. Even if hurt, you believe they are capable of honesty, accountability, and care.

Consider letting go if:
- There is no genuine apology and accountability for either of your actions.
- The relationship consistently drains you. You feel more anxious, heavy, or diminished after interactions than uplifted.
- Respect has been broken. Disregard for boundaries, repeated betrayal, or lack of accountability erodes the foundation of trust.
- Your peace is consistently disrupted. If the connection brings more chaos, confusion and conflict than care, release may be the healthiest option.

If you decide to end the friendship, and if it is physically and emotionally safe to do so (meaning, it will not further traumatize you), try to prioritize ending things in a direct and considerate way. This could be in person, over the phone, or even by text—whatever feels most appropriate. The goal is to provide both of you with the clarity you deserve, so that neither of you is left to guess or wonder. I think it is also important to note that while we may go into the conversation hoping to rebuild the relationship, or at least gain some closure, the other person may or may not be willing and ready to do the same; and we need to respect where they are in their own healing journey. This is not an invitation to continue reaching out over and over until you get a response. This is an opportunity to redirect some of your energy back to yourself, and your own healing and self-care.

The gift of clarity is liberating. It can ease the weight of the guilt that often accompanies friendship breakups, regardless of how or why they end. Guilt and remorse are uncomfortable feelings, and it is natural to experience them in situations like this; but experiencing guilt does not mean you are a bad person or that you have made the wrong choice by ending the friendship. This kind of guilt says, "I loved them, and it hurts to have to let them go."

Mirror Moment (Write & Reflect): What is your conflict style? What conversation are you avoiding? Who in your life have you lost without the chance for closure, and how has that impacted you? If you allowed yourself to grieve this friendship honestly, what might that grief need from you to feel complete?

_____

_____

_____

_____

_____

_____

_____

_____

_____

_____

_____

_____

_____

_____

_____

_____

_____

_____

Girlfriend Gem Exercise: Friendship Eulogy or Letter I'll Never Send

This is your safe space to put your emotions into words—no judgment, no performance, just truth. You can choose one or both of the exercises: *The Friendship Eulogy*, or *The Letter I'll Never Send*.

The Friendship Eulogy: Imagine you are giving a heartfelt tribute to the friendship you once had. This is not about bashing or sugarcoating—it is about honoring what was real. You might include:

When and how you met

Your favorite shared memories

What this friendship meant to you at its best

What you have learned from knowing them

What you will miss most

Any final words you would want to leave with them in your heart

The Letter I'll Never Send: Write directly to your friend, letting every emotional truth have a voice—joy, sadness, anger, confusion, gratitude. Remember: This letter is for your eyes only, not theirs. Do not worry about grammar, spelling, or making it "sound good." If you get stuck, try writing "I feel…" or "I wish…" and see where it takes you. Pause if emotions feel too heavy, and return when you feel ready. When you are finished, take a breath. You just gave your feelings a home outside of your body. You may choose to rip it up and throw it away, or you may decide to burn it (safely in a fireplace, or contained space outside that will not cause harm to any person, space, or thing). If you decide to write a separate letter that you actually want to give to your friend, make sure it is from a place of healing, not harm. If you find yourself going full roast mode, keep it in your journal—we are here for healing, not smoke, sis!

Crown Check Affirmation:

Not every friendship is meant to last forever, but every friendship teaches me something. Choosing to address conflict and to walk away in peace are acts of self-respect and love.

Soul Sista Soundtrack:

Good Mourning by India.Arie

PART FOUR: Summer
Reunions, Second Chances, and Self-Care

Chapter 11:

Healing the Rift: Tools for Having the Hard Conversations

Before approaching a difficult conversation with a sister friend, it is essential to ground ourselves emotionally—reflecting on our feelings, and clarifying what our hopes are in having this conversation. We may ask ourselves, am I seeking understanding, reconciliation, or healthy boundaries? Centering our intentions allows the dialogue to be focused and healing rather than reactive. We have to remember to give ourselves permission to feel fully, and without judgment.

It is also necessary to reflect on and be honest about the role we may have played in the strain on the friendship. This can honestly be one of the most challenging aspects to reflect on. It is not easy to face ourselves to own up to the impact of our behaviors and choices, but it is absolutely necessary. Even if we genuinely feel we did nothing wrong, we might still benefit from asking ourselves, why did I stay in this friendship, or what was going on in/around me to impact my decision to be in relationship with this person?

Reflection and journaling help integrate the knowledge we gain from these moments. Writing helps us identify patterns in our own responses, clarify needs, and reinforce self-awareness. The goal is growth, not perfection—learning how to communicate honestly while preserving the love and safety that define Black women's sisterhood.

Quick Checklist for Hard Conversations:

- Ground yourself: name your emotions and intentions.
- Choose a safe time and space. It's best to avoid crowded, or noisy spaces. Ideally, the space will be neutral ground where both/all parties feel safe.
- Use "I" statements to express feelings. "I feel..." "I was hurt by..."
- Listen actively and validate without judgment. Avoid interrupting or talking over one another. Try your best to be understanding and empathetic.
- Take responsibility and apologize where needed. Be genuine. Resist the urge to become defensive. It does not hurt anything but your ego to simply say, "I apologize." The focus should be on relationship repair, not an attempt to prove your point.
- Set boundaries for emotional safety. If part of the reason for the rift in the relationship was due to boundaries being crossed, clearly state the boundary, and the action you will take if the boundary continues to be crossed. For example, "If you continue to call me and gossip about others, I will tell you I am not going to engage in gossip, and I will end the call."
- Plan small acts of repair or follow-up. For example, if you agree to weekly text check-ins, remain committed and consistent with the established line of communication.
- Reflect and journal afterward to integrate learning.

• • • • • • • • • • • • • • • •

Mirror Moment (Write & Reflect): Take a moment to think about a conversation you might have been avoiding with a sister-friend. In the space below, write out some talking points you would like to discuss with her in preparation for the conversation, using the tips and tools we discussed in this chapter.

_____

_____

_____

_____

_____

_____

_____

_____

_____

_____

_____

_____

_____

_____

_____

_____

_____

Girlfriend Gem Exercise: Bridge Building Script

Take 5–10 minutes to write whatever comes to mind about the conflict. Some of the things you might write about could be:

What hurt me most in this situation?

What role did I play in the disagreement?

What do I wish my friend understood about my experience?

_____

_____

_____

_____

_____

_____

_____

_____

_____

_____

_____

_____

_____

_____

_____

_____

_____

_____

_____

_____

_____

_____

_____

_____

_____

_____

Write Your Script: **Begin the script with an acknowledgment of your bond. You might say:** "I value our friendship and the history we share…" Use "I" statements to express your feelings without blame: "I felt hurt when…" Include a statement about your needs or intentions: "I want us to find understanding and restore trust…"

_____

_____

_____

_____

_____

_____

_____

_____

_____

_____

_____

_____

_____

_____

_____

_____

_____

Empathize: Add a paragraph imagining your friend's perspective. Example: "I imagine you may have felt overwhelmed or misunderstood, and I want to hear your side without judgment/take accountability for how I contributed to that."

_____

_____

_____

_____

_____

_____

_____

_____

Reflect Post-Conversation: After the conversation, reflect on the following:

What did I learn about myself?

How did this conversation shift my perspective?

What actions can I take to nurture this friendship moving forward?

Crown Check Affirmation:

I speak truth with love, I listen with openness, and I honor the bond we share. Our friendship can grow through honesty and care.

Soul Sista Soundtrack:

You Are My Friend by Sylvester

Chapter 12:

Apologies and Forgiveness

Apologies and forgiveness can be such bittersweet practices, partly because both tend to carry a sense of mystery for many of us. If we are being honest, some of us have never truly received a genuine apology that we deserved; and some of us have never learned how to apologize and forgive.

When it comes to clearing up common misconceptions about forgiveness, I think it's easiest to start by identifying what forgiveness is not. To forgive is not to excuse. It does not mean pretending harm never happened or forcing reconciliation with someone who remains unsafe. It does not require us to forget the wrongdoing, but we can remember without being chained to bitterness. Forgiveness also does not mean automatic reconciliation. Rebuilding a relationship requires mutual trust, a change in behavior, and a sense of safety. Forgiveness is an inward release, regardless of whether or not reconciliation is possible.

Forgiveness does not always bring instant relief of emotional heaviness. It sometimes unfolds in phases of anger, grief, clarity, and release. Some days we feel free; other days, we revisit the pain. Both are part of the process. Forgiving someone (or being forgiven yourself) does not mean that pain disappears or that feelings are no longer valid once we have extended forgiveness. Forgiveness helps us ensure the offense no longer has power over us—it does not erase the feelings themselves. To forgive is to loosen the grip of resentment on our nervous system, thoughts, and heart. It is choosing not to let someone else's harm dictate the pace of our healing.

In short, forgiveness means:

> Allowing ourselves to grieve what was lost.
> Creating space for joy, even while wounds remain tender.
> Releasing the illusion that the past could be undone.

Apologies are bridges—not guarantees—to forgiveness. A genuine apology should include what I call the *Three A's:*

1. Acknowledgment of the specific harm.
2. Accountability without excuses or blame-shifting.
3. Action that demonstrates real change in our behaviors that caused harm.

When apologies never come—or arrive shallow and incomplete—it is natural to feel disappointment, betrayal, or grief. If left unaddressed, unforgiveness can become resentment. Resentment, when carried for too long, keeps the nervous system in a state of fight-or-flight mode. It fuels constant defensiveness, which can block the creation or repair of healthy, meaningful friendships.

Practices rooted in mindfulness—such as deep breathing, grounding rituals, storytelling, and boundary-setting—can soothe the body and remind us that safety is still possible in friendships.

● ● ● ● ● ● ● ● ● ● ● ● ● ● ● ● ●

Mirror Moment (Write & Reflect): What cultural or family beliefs about forgiveness have shaped you and your approach to navigating friendship repair? Which do you want to keep, and which are you ready to let go of?

_____

_____

_____

_____

_____

_____

_____

_____

_____

_____

_____

_____

_____

Girlfriend Gem Exercise: Forgiveness Meditation

1. Close your eyes and picture the friend you need to forgive at a distance.
2. Imagine a heavy rope connecting you.
3. With each exhale, see the strands unraveling.
4. You may choose to let the rope fall—or witness it loosening without forcing release.

Crown Check Affirmation:

Forgiveness is not about erasing what happened; it's about letting go and reclaiming myself from what happened.

Soul Sista Soundtrack:

Before I Let Go by Beyoncé

Chapter 13:

Rebuilding Healthy Connections

Rebuilding friendships reflects and affirms the divinity of Black women's connections, where truth-telling and accountability coexist with grace and tenderness. Choosing to re-enter friendships after rupture resists the harmful narratives that Black women must always be silent; or worse, that we cannot get along. Instead, it declares: our wholeness, our bonds, and our healing matter. In a world that often fragments Black women's communities, friendship repair is freedom. It interrupts internalized messages that we are disposable or unworthy of deep care and attention.

As I emphasized in Chapter Eleven, upon making the decision to rebuild our friendships, it is essential to engage in honest self-reflection before reaching out to our friend. This includes reflecting on what worked and what didn't work in the past, and taking responsibility for our part in any past issues without over-criticizing ourselves. After sitting in the introspection, we can communicate honestly and kindly.

The following are practical tips to help us move toward healing our friendships after the conflict has been addressed:

1. Listen as much as you speak. Ask how they have been and what they need from you. Address any lingering tension directly but gently—clarity builds trust.

2. Rebuild slowly and consistently. Do not rush the process; rebuilding trust takes time. Begin with small, positive interactions, such as check-ins, shared activities, or brief conversations. Consistency matters more than intensity.

3. Establish healthy boundaries. Be mindful of emotional limits—both yours and theirs. Respect each other's time, privacy, and energy. A healthy friendship strikes a balance between closeness and individuality.

4. Bring gratitude and positivity. Express appreciation for them and for the chance to reconnect. Focus on shared values and good memories rather than past mistakes. Celebrate small steps in the healing process.

5. Allow space for change. People grow, and the friendship may look different now—and that's OK. Accept that not everything will return to its former state. Stay curious about who each other has become.

6. Practice forgiveness for them, and for yourself. Let go of resentment or self-blame where possible.

Mirror Moment (Write & Reflect): When you think about rebuilding a friendship, what do you need to feel safe, seen, and valued—and how can you offer those same things to your friends?

_____

_____

_____

_____

_____

_____

_____

_____

_____

_____

_____

_____

_____

_____

_____

_____

Girlfriend Gem Exercise: A Body Check-in on Friendship Safety

Take a few moments to notice how your body responds when you think about friendships where you feel safe, seen, and valued.

1. Sit comfortably. Take three slow, deep breaths. Place one hand on your heart and the other on your stomach.

2. Bring to mind a friendship where you feel genuinely cared for. Picture a moment of laughter, honesty, or support with this friend.

3. As you sit with this memory, gently scan your body. Ask yourself:

    What do I feel in my chest—tightness, expansion, ease?

    How does my breath flow—shallow or steady?

    Do I feel warmth, tingling, lightness, or calm in any areas?

    Where do I sense release, and where do I sense holding back?

4. Write about what safety in friendship feels like in your body. Some guiding questions to help you reflect: When I feel safe with a friend, how does my body signal this to me? What practices or boundaries help me feel grounded in that safety? How can I honor these signals moving forward in my friendships?

_____

_____

_____

_____

_____

_____

_____

_____

_____

_____

_____

_____

_____

_____

_____

_____

_____

Crown Check Affirmation:

I honor the power of repair. Rebuilding friendship is not a step backward, but an act of courage, love, and liberation.

Soul Sista Soundtrack:

That's What Friends Are For by Dionne Warwick, Gladys Knight, Stevie Wonder & Elton John

Chapter 14:

Healing Ourselves After Friendship Breakups

I wanted to ensure that a chapter was explicitly dedicated to the practice of healing ourselves in the aftermath of friendship breakups. When we end things with our former friends, we may find ourselves navigating feelings of grief, sadness, and confusion. For some of us, there may even be some feelings of relief. Some of us may experience disappointment from our own choices and/or the choices of our former friends that have hurt us. The goal then becomes allowing ourselves to feel it all, instead of bottling it up, and to avoid leaning deeply into self-disparaging beliefs—but instead, leaning into self-compassion.

In *Matters of the Heart: Healing Your Relationship with Yourself and Those You Love*, Dr. Thema Bryant says, "Self-compassion requires not only self-forgiveness but also liberation from perfectionism." This quote resonated with me. It speaks to the essence of what some of us experience as the extremely high standards we put on ourselves when things don't work out. Dr. Bryant goes on to say:

"This is vital, because when you believe in false dichotomies—you are either a total success or a complete failure—then whenever you make a mistake, fall short, or live

in a way that you were trying to break free from, you will start to think of yourself as a failure. You will create impossible standards for yourself, and as a result, think of yourself solely in a negative light when, in reality, you're in a process of growth and change, as we all are. You are healing, transforming, climbing, and shifting, Yes!?!"

Here are some steps that are necessary to heal ourselves after the friendship ends:

1. Allow space to grieve. Name the loss. Acknowledge that it is a loss. Give yourself permission to feel. Sadness, anger, confusion, and relief are all normal. Do not minimize it because it's "just a friend."

2. Reflect without blame. Avoid replaying every detail. Reflection helps with growth, but rumination keeps us stuck. Recognize mutual humanity—that we're all doing the best with what we have at the time.

3. Create closure, even if it has to be one-sided. Have an honest conversation to express gratitude or clarify misunderstandings. If direct contact is not safe or possible, try journaling to release lingering emotions. Create a releasing ritual, like lighting a candle, or going for a symbolic walk.

4. Reconnect with yourself. Reinvest in personal joy. Revisit hobbies, interests, or routines that make you feel like yourself. Reclaim your emotional energy. Friendships often intertwine identities; find yourself again outside that dynamic. Spend time with supportive people who ground and uplift you.

5. Talk to yourself kindly. Healing takes time—it's not a linear process. Avoid labeling the breakup as a failure. Affirm your worthiness of love and connection.

6. Set boundaries for healing. Limit social media exposure if seeing them triggers pain. Give yourself permission to say no to mutual social situations while you're still tender. Protect your emotional space.

7. Once the grief softens, allow yourself to trust again. Seek new or deepened friendships that align with your current season of life. Remember: endings make room for beginnings.

Mirror Moment (Write & Reflect): What are you ready to let go of so you can move forward with peace? What does healing look like for you right now—emotionally, mentally, or spiritually?

_____

_____

_____

_____

_____

_____

_____

_____

_____

_____

_____

_____

_____

_____

_____

_____

Girlfriend Gem Exercise: My Friendship Manifesto

Take a few quiet minutes to reflect on your values, needs, and hopes in your friendships. Write down statements (as long or as short as you want/need them to be) that capture how you want to show up for your friends and how you want to be treated. Keep it personal, empowering, and positive.

Example:
Stephanie's Friendship Manifesto:

I will listen.
Truly listen, with ears and heart wide open,
Without rushing to fix, explain, or defend.
I will hold space for your pain, your laughter, your silences,
Knowing that your story matters as much as mine.

I will speak my truth.
Even when my voice shakes,
Even when it feels heavy,
Even when it risks the bond we share.
I will speak gently, but firmly,
My voice is part of the love I bring.

I will honor boundaries.
I will recognize my own limits,
And respect yours.
I will not over-give until I am empty,
And I will not ask you to do what feels unsafe.

I will celebrate you.
In your victories, big and small,

In your breakthroughs, your growth, your healing,
I will cheer you on,
Because your joy is my joy, too.

I will forgive.
Not always quickly, not always easily,
But I will remember that we are human,
Learning, stumbling, reaching.
I will forgive the mistakes, the misunderstandings.

I will ask for help.
I will lean in when I need to lean in.
I will not carry alone what is meant for shared shoulders.
I will let you hold me, as I hold you.

I will nurture our bond.
Through calls, texts, hugs, visits, and check-ins.
Through honesty, patience, and empathy.
Through disagreement, reflection, and growth.
Through it all, I will tend to this garden of sisterhood,
Knowing that it flourishes only with intention, care, and love.

I will love myself in this process.
I will protect my heart, my voice, my joy,
So that I can show up fully for you, for us.

I promise, here, in these words,
To honor friendship as a gift,
I promise to bring my best self,
To honor yours,
And together, to walk this path of sisterhood.

Crown Check Affirmation:

I welcome the lessons of accountability, the grace of forgiveness, and the joy of renewed connection. I am worthy of friendships that heal, grow, and reflect my wholeness.

Soul Sista Soundtrack:

Womanifesto by Jill Scott

Chapter 15:

Self-Reflection and Growth

I have spent a lot of time reflecting on the friendships I have been blessed to experience, as well as the pain of those that have shifted, distanced, or ended. I have also turned inward to consider who I am as a friend and the ways I can grow.

One lesson that has stood out is the importance of learning to love my friends in the ways that matter most to them—not just defaulting to what comes naturally for me. Often, this means paying closer attention to their love languages, with the intention of making them feel truly seen and cared for. Honestly, this is not always easy. Navigating life as a wife, mom, therapist, caregiver, soror, and more can make that level of attunement feel overwhelming. Still, I remind myself that it is not about doing everything perfectly. It is about showing intention, prioritizing quality over quantity, and managing my own life in ways that reduce overwhelm—including asking for help when I need it, so I am not carrying more than I can hold.

This kind of self-reflection has been healing—for me and for some of my closest friendships. It has encouraged me to show up with more grace, to be fully myself, and to meet my sister-friends where they are—whether that means sharing in joy, holding space for sorrow, navigating moments of anger, or simply being together in silence.

Every friendship—whether it lasts a season or a lifetime—leaves an imprint. The difficult ones teach resilience, clarity, and boundaries. The nourishing ones remind us that joy, laughter, and deep connection are possible. Both prepare us to welcome healthier, more life-giving friendships in the future.

Tough conversations between Black women friends are acts of reclamation. These dialogues become sacred spaces where truth-telling interrupts patterns of silence that have historically been imposed on Black women. Speaking openly, even at the risk of conflict or loss, affirms our right to be fully seen and heard. These moments embody radical love—insisting that our wholeness matters and that nurturing authentic sisterhood is a form of communal healing. Whether a friendship is repaired or released, engaging with honesty honors the self. It affirms the dignity of the women involved.

Healing is not just individual, but collective. By naming our truths in friendship, we resist internalized oppression and reclaim our agency. Growth is not solely dependent on the outcome of a relationship, but on the freedom gained from acting with authenticity, courage, and care. In this way, self-reflection becomes a liberatory practice, teaching us that our value does not rest on preserving every connection, but on honoring the lessons each one brings.

Mirror Moment (Write & Reflect): In what ways has navigating the seasons of your sisterhoods helped you to grow as a friend? As a person?

_____

_____

_____

_____

_____

_____

_____

Girlfriend Gem Exercise: Friendship Self-Inventory

This self-inventory is a tool to help you identify your strengths as a friend and areas where you have room for growth. Read through each category. Circle "S" for strength, or "G" for growth, based on where you are in your friendships right now.

Strength: "I consistently embody this in my friendships."
Growth Area: "This is something I am working on, or want to improve."

		1. Communication & Honesty
S	G	I speak openly and honestly with my friends.
S	G	I listen without interrupting or dismissing.
S	G	I can engage in challenging conversations with care and consideration.
S	G	I honor my friends' truths, even when they differ from mine.
		2. Presence & Support
S	G	I celebrate my friends' wins with joy, not comparison.
S	G	I show up when my friends need me—emotionally, spiritually, or practically.
S	G	I check in regularly, even when life gets busy.
S	G	I offer grace and understanding when my friends are going through a tough time.

3. Boundaries & Accountability

S	G	
S	G	I clearly communicate my needs and limits.
S	G	I respect my friends' boundaries without taking it personally.
S	G	I take responsibility when I have caused harm.
S	G	I welcome feedback without defensiveness.

4. Reciprocity & Mutual Care

S	G	
S	G	I give support without keeping score.
S	G	I allow myself to receive care, not just give it.
S	G	I notice when a friendship feels unbalanced and address it.
S	G	I value mutual growth over one-sidedness.

5. Liberation & Healing in Friendship

S	G	
S	G	I challenge oppressive patterns (such as silence, comparison, and self-sacrifice) within myself and in my relationships.
S	G	I affirm my friends' identities and lived experiences.
S	G	I nurture friendships that value authenticity over performance.
S	G	I view tough conversations as opportunities for reflection and healing, not just conflict.

Reflection Questions:

1. Looking at your strengths and areas for growth, where do you feel most grounded as a friend?
2. Which "growth areas" feel most urgent for you right now?
3. What support, practices, or affirmations could help you strengthen these areas?

_____

_____

_____

_____

_____

_____

_____

_____

_____

_____

_____

_____

_____

_____

_____

_____

_____

Crown Check Affirmation:

I open myself to rediscovering who I am, and to loving myself back to wholeness.

Soul Sista Soundtrack:

No More Drama by Mary J. Blige

Chapter 16:

Creating a Friendship Legacy

When I look at my daughter, I often find myself daydreaming about the friendships that will shape her life. Even now, at just three years old, she has her "day-ones"—her best friends. These three girls have been side by side since they were in strollers, and now they toddle through the world together, learning, laughing, and discovering in unison. Watching them, I can't help but ask myself: What kind of example am I setting? What legacy of friendship am I leaving for my daughter to inherit?

I think back to my own childhood and the legacy of my mother. I remember her circle of sister-friends—women who showed up for one another. Their bond was not only a source of strength for each other but also a living lesson for me, teaching me what friendship looks like.

Now, as I stand in the place my mother once stood, I feel the weight and the gift of that inheritance, because friendship is not just about companionship—it is about building community, cultivating belonging, and teaching the next generation that love and connection extend beyond family lines. My daughter will learn how to nurture her own friendships; not just from her besties, but from the way she watches me love and honor the women I call friends.

This is why it matters that we pause to reflect. We—the aunts, the mothers, the sister-friends—are rearing a new generation. These little ones are watching how we treat one another, how we celebrate, how we forgive, how we show up, and even how we bow out intentionally. One day, they will imitate what they have seen.

So when I look at my daughter and her sweet friends, I pray that my example plants seeds: seeds of loyalty, generosity, and joy in her friendships. Seeds of women who will hold one another up in the hardest seasons, and cheer one another on in the brightest ones. The true legacy of friendship is so much more than the memories we make with our own sister-friends—it is the way we shape the bonds of those who are coming after us. We are building a lineage of love, one friendship at a time.

Mirror Moment (Write & Reflect): How do your friendships reflect your larger journey of healing and liberation?

_____

_____

_____

_____

_____

_____

_____

_____

_____

_____

_____

Girlfriend Gem Exercise: The Friendship Legacy Tree

As you look at the *Friendship Legacy Tree*, take a moment to reflect on your own friendship legacy. Think about the women whose love and example rooted you, the values that form your trunk, the younger ones who grow from your branches, and the lessons you hope will live on through your leaves. Write a few words or sentences capturing what you want the next generation of Black women to know about friendship, and finish with this thought: "The legacy I want to leave through my friendships is…"

THE HEALTH
OF OUR
FRIENDSHIPS
The Leaves

MY FRIENDS
The Branches

ME
The Trunk

THE FRIENDSHIP TREE

Crown Check Affirmation:

I create a legacy of sisterhood, showing the next generation the true power of sisterhood.

Soul Sista Soundtrack:

I'm Every Woman by Chaka Khan

References

Bradford, J. H. (2023). Sisterhood Heals: The transformative power of healing in community. Random House.

Bryant, T. (2025). Matters of the Heart: Healing your relationship with yourself and those you love. Penguin.

hooks, b. (2001). All About Love: New visions. William Morrow.

Additional Resources to Continue Your Sisterhood Healing Journey

Books

Collins, P. H. (2000). Black Feminist Thought: Knowledge, consciousness, and the politics of empowerment. Routledge.

Knowles-Lawson, T. & O'Leary, K. C. (2025). Matriarch: A memoir. One World.

Lorde, A. (2007). Sister Outsider: Essays and speeches. Crossing Press.

Tawwab, N. G. (2021). Set Boundaries, Find Peace: A guide to reclaiming yourself. TarcherPerigee.

Walker, A. (1982). The Color Purple. Pocket Books.

Podcasts

1. Healed Girl Era Podcast with Gia Peppers
2. Gettin' Grown Podcast with Jade and Keia
3. Therapy for Black Girls Podcast with Dr. Joy Harden Bradford

4. Mind Ya Mental Podcast with Dr. Raquel Martin
5. IRL (In Real Life) Podcast with Angie Martinez
6. You Need to Hear This Podcast with Nedra Glover Tawwab
7. Homecoming Podcast with Dr. Thema Bryant
8. Jill Scott Presents: J.ILL the Podcast with Jill Scott, Aja Grayden Dantzler and Laiya St. Clair
9. Friend Fusion with Trinity Mitchell
10. Truth's Table

Social Media

1. Girl-Trek
2. She Is Seen Collective
3. The Sister Circle Collective
4. Your Friend Trin
5. Melanin and Mental Health
6. Black Girls Smile

ACKNOWLEDGMENTS

Dear God, I thank you for giving me the ability to write, to think, and for the wisdom and insight to bring this book to fruition. Thank you for the message you placed on my heart. Let it be nourishment for the souls of my sisters.

Thank you to my family for your patience throughout my writing and publishing process. Thank you for your encouragement and support. BJ, Kia, mom, dad, MIL, I love you immensely.

Thank you to my sister-friends. Our conversations and relationships have been a significant part of the inspiration for writing this book. You motivate and encourage me daily to be the best version of myself, and for that, I am forever grateful. I love you.